The Period Book

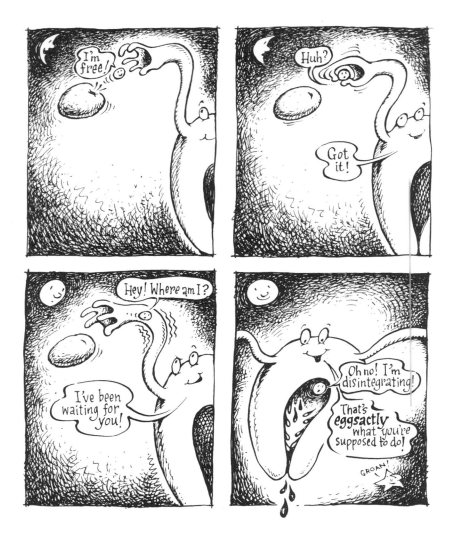

Updated Edition, including new information on body image

The Period Book

Everything You Don't Want to Ask
(But Need to Know)

BY KAREN GRAVELLE &
JENNIFER GRAVELLE

Illustrations by Debbie Palen

WALKER & COMPANY
NEW YORK

To our mothers, Aileen and Jane Gravelle

First published in the United States of America in 1996 by Walker Publishing Company, Inc.
Updated edition published in 2006

For information about permission to reproduce selections from
this book, write to Permissions, Walker & Company,
104 Fifth Avenue, New York, New York 10011

The Library of Congress has cataloged the earlier edition as follows:
Gravelle, Karen.
The period book : everything you don't want to ask (but need to know) / by Karen Gravelle & Jennifer
Gravelle ; illustrations by Debbie Palen.
p. cm.
Includes index.
Summary: Explains what happens at the onset of menstruation,
discussing what to wear, going to the gynecologist, and how to handle various problems.
ISBN-10: 0-8027-8420-8 • ISBN-13: 978-0-8027-8420-9 (hardcover)
ISBN-10: 0-8027-7478-4 • ISBN-13:978-0-8027-7478-1 (paperback)
1. Menstruation—Juvenile literature. [1. Menstruation.]
I. Gravelle, Jennifer. II. Palen, Debbie, ill. III. Title.
QP263.G73 1996
612.6′62—dc20   95-31101

ISBN-10: 0-8027-8072-5 • ISBN-13: 978-0-8027-8072-0 (updated hardcover)
ISBN-10: 0-8027-7736-8 • ISBN-13: 978-0-8027-7736-2 (updated paperback)

Book design by Chris Welch

Visit Walker & Company's Web site at www.walkeryoungreaders.com

Printed in the United States of America
10

All papers used by Walker & Company are natural, recyclable products
made from wood grown in well-managed forests. The manufacturing processes
conform to the environmental regulations of the country of origin.

Contents

Acknowledgments

A lot of people—men as well as women—helped us in writing this book. We would like to thank these very special consultants for sharing their thoughts, feelings, experiences, and expertise with us: Erin Boccio, Denise Cammarata, Lisa Cammarata, Elizabeth Goveia, Aileen Gravelle, Jane Gravelle, Dr. Radoslav Jovanovic, Sue Ellen Sherblom, Thomas Woodward, and Chris Young.

A Note from Jennifer

When my aunt, Karen Gravelle, asked me to help her with this book, I agreed immediately. I think the more books on the market about getting your period, the better. The only other way you can learn about this subject is from your mother or in school. I was lucky because my mom and I could talk about the topic. I know for most girls, it's pretty embarrassing to talk in public about getting your period. Many girls think they'll look stupid if they don't know something, so they can be afraid to ask questions—particularly if the question sounds kind of dumb, like, "What happens if you can't get a tampon out?"

My aunt and I wanted to answer questions that girls my age would like to ask but are afraid to. Chapter 8, "What If . . . ?" is my favorite part of the book. These are the sort of things you want to know about, but you probably won't bring up in a class.

We also hope that this book will help parents and daughters talk about menstruation and sex. I know a lot of girls have trouble discussing these topics with their parents. I'd just like to say to parents that you shouldn't think about it as The Talk. Think of it as a conversation that you may have with your daughter again and again. There's never a good time for The Talk, but there's always time for a conversation.

Jennifer Gravelle
(age 15, March 1995)

A Note to Parents

In the ten years since *The Period Book* first came out, Jenny and I have been asked by many parents for some tips on how to talk to their daughters about puberty. Obviously, introducing the topic of puberty to a nine-year-old is very different from helping a fourteen-year-old deal with her anxiety about not having started to menstruate. Nevertheless, we felt there is some advice for parents that will prove useful, regardless of where your daughter is in this process.

Sort Out Your Own Feelings First

Most parents experience a variety of emotions when their child enters puberty. To make sure that these feelings don't get in the way of negotiating this new terrain with your daughter, take a little time to sort out your own emotions before trying to help her with hers. In the process, you may find that some of your feelings are very similar to those she is having—a realization that can be reassuring when it seems that you two inhabit different planets.

Parents usually feel some sense of loss as their child begins to move into adolescence. Just as you mourn the end of her childhood, your daughter may be grieving this loss herself. However, while you are likely to understand the cause of your feelings, she may have more difficulty recognizing—much less admitting—that this could be the source of some of the sadness she feels from time to time.

A girl's first period also entails another loss—that of the carefree, unself-conscious relationship she has experienced with her body until now. From this point on, she will have to monitor her body in a way that is unique to women. She will have to learn, and continually keep in mind, the timing of her own particular monthly cycle so that she will know when to expect her period. During her period, she will have to be careful to keep tampons and/or pads on hand. And, whether it ever happens or not, she will have to guard against the possibility of menstrual blood seeping through her clothing and embarrassing her. In one way or another, even if it's just planning what to bring on a future camping trip, her period will always be a consideration.

The truth is that periods—and everything they involve—can be a drag. So, it's only natural if you feel a little sad that your daughter will have to deal with all of it from now on, especially if she is only nine or ten years old. And if she's the only one among her friends who has to struggle with these issues, she's likely to be a little sad, and probably a little angry, too.

Speaking of anger, if your daughter is particularly young when she gets her first period, you may feel some resentment at being forced to deal with her adolescence before *you* are ready. The elementary school years generally provide a break for parents between the constant caregiving of the preschool years and the turmoil of adolescence. So, it may seem to you that your daughter is not the only one being cheated out of this relatively carefree time. Just remember that this is no more her fault than it is yours.

For parents, the most frightening aspect of adolescence is the decreasing control they have over their child's behavior. Just when your daughter's new independence and increasing mobility make it possible for her to get into real trouble, your ability to protect her from making serious mistakes begins to evaporate. Regardless of how old your daughter is when she begins to menstruate, or how interested she may or may not be in having sex, her first period is likely to trigger your concerns about casual sex, unwanted pregnancy, sexually transmitted diseases, and rape.

Ironically, your daughter is also dealing with an unnerving loss of control, although in her case, the control is over her own developing body. It's a rare girl indeed whose body changes in a manner and at a rate with which she's comfortable. In addition to having no influence over these changes, she has little ability to gauge whether they are "normal." Most adults have mercifully forgotten, or actively repressed, how nervous and worried they were about this whole process. As a result, concerns that are very real to her may seem silly to you. It goes without saying that if you want her to confide in you, it's important to take these concerns seriously.

Keep Your Expectations Realistic

In talking with your daughter, it can be easy to forget what you're trying to achieve and instead get caught up in "doing it right." Remember, your goals here are pretty simple: (1) to give her the information she needs and (2) to let her know that you are there for her and are willing and able to help with her questions, concerns, and feelings about puberty and menstruation. If you succeed in accomplishing this, then you've done your job. With some luck, she'll be eager to confide in you. But if she isn't, it doesn't mean that you've failed somehow.

The ease with which you two are able to talk about these things will depend on several things, including her personality, age, and developmental level, as well as the kind of relationship the two of you have had. For example, if your daughter is a very private child who doesn't open up easily, it's unlikely that she will be any more at ease discussing puberty. Even if she has always been comfortable sharing her feelings and concerns with you, this may change as she approaches puberty. After all, one of the jobs of being an adolescent is to separate from your parents, so it's natural for her to become increasingly ambivalent about discussing very personal matters with you.

If you're like many parents, there will be some uncomfortable moments as you and your daughter begin to talk about puberty and menstruation. Fortunately, these discussions are part of an ongoing process, not a one-shot deal. So give yourself a break. Even if your first attempts are awkward, you'll have plenty of opportunities to improve.

Talking with Your Daughter

Seize the Moment

Answer your daughter's questions and address her concerns when she raises them, not later, even if this is not the most convenient time for you. For all you know, she may have spent the last two days trying to figure out how to broach the subject with you. If it really isn't feasible for you to talk at the moment, set up a time later that day when the two of you can sit down together. If you don't know the answer to a question she asks, admit that you're unclear about it and suggest that the two of you find the answer together. Making it a joint project can defuse some of the awkwardness she (or you) may feel and presents an opportunity for her to raise other questions.

Be Alert to Hidden Questions

You've had decades to absorb this information, but most or all of it may be new to your daughter. It's a lot to learn all at once, and she may need to have certain things explained to her several times. However, repeating the same questions over and over can be a sign that something else is going on. Adolescents can be so worried that something abnormal is happening to them that they are afraid to ask for fear their suspicions will be confirmed. As a result, they may try to get information indirectly by asking questions that are only peripherally related to their real concerns. Since these attempts are often unsuccessful, they may ask the question again in the hope that this time, the answer they're looking for will be included somewhere. If you have the sense that this may be the case, say so. Comment that it seems that you're not really giving her the information she needs, and ask if there is something that is bothering her.

A Little Humor Goes a Long Way

   Never underestimate the value of humor in helping your daughter deal with puberty. As luck would have it, menstruation provides a virtually unlimited source of embarrassing moments that can be mined for a good laugh. Sharing the humor in your own past experiences is a good way to establish a relaxed environment and can be very effective in reducing potentially mortifying puberty-related events to manageable proportions.

Using *The Period Book*

At the risk of stating the obvious, an important first step in using *The Period Book* is to read it yourself. Although you may have had decades of hands-on experience as a menstruating woman, you'll probably learn some things you didn't know before. I know I did! One of the book's most useful functions is as a common ground for conversations between you and your daughter, but that works only if both of you have read the material.

   If you're a father, reading the book will also help you to help your daughter. While many, if not most, men feel uncomfortable taking an active role in talking to their daughters about the physical changes of puberty, dads can be a great source of support in guiding their daughters through the emotional and social pitfalls of adolescence. However, since some of a girl's concerns are specific to being a woman, it's important that fathers have a working knowledge of what puberty is like for a girl. *The Period Book* will give you an insider's perspective.

Finally, regardless of how you use *The Period Book*, it should be as part of an ongoing dialogue that you and your daughter have about growing up—not as a substitute for face-to-face conversations. When you discuss puberty and menstruation, your daughter's reaction may vary from eye-rolling to eager sharing, but it's critical that you demonstrate a willingness and an ability to talk about these issues. She may or may not use your help directly, but knowing that it is there, and that she can count on it, will make all the difference. And chances are that she'll rely on your guidance more than you realize.

The Period Book

introduction

As you can tell from the title, this book is about getting your period—what a period is, why it happens, what it feels like, and what to do when you get it. But more important, this book is about changes, since the reason a girl gets a period in the first place is that her body is changing from a child's body into a woman's body. The time when these changes are occurring is called puberty.

It's a funny thing, but most of us aren't completely comfortable with changes, even when they are something we really want. The problem is that we often don't have much say over *when* they happen. It can be hard when things change before we're ready for them to change—or after we've been ready for ages! This is particularly true when the change is an

important one, like starting junior high or middle school. It's even more true when what's changing is your own body.

So if you're not quite sure how you feel about these changes, you're not alone. Some girls can hardly wait to get their period, while others would be very happy to wait a little longer. Many girls feel one way on some days and the opposite on others.

Although you can't control when you first get your period, knowing what to expect helps make things much easier. This book will tell you what to expect not only with your period but with all the other changes happening in your body. Some of these changes you may already have noticed, so let's start with them.

·1·

Changes of Puberty

Those You Can See

If you look at a classroom of sixth or seventh graders, you'll notice something strange. When they were in the third grade, these boys and girls were pretty much the same height. But now that they're eleven or twelve years old, the girls are generally taller than the boys. What happened?

Growth Spurt

The answer is that many of the sixth-grade girls have entered their growth spurt, one of the first signs of puberty. When both boys and girls are

younger, they grow at the rate of about two inches a year. But when girls enter puberty, they start growing much faster, sometimes as much as four inches a year.

Of course, boys go through puberty as well in order to develop into men. But they usually don't start their growth spurt until they are a little older. So for a few years, the girls are taller than the boys. When boys finally start growing in their mid to late teens, they generally become taller than girls.

Getting taller isn't the only thing that happens during the growth spurt. Arms, legs, and feet also begin growing much faster. In fact, feet are likely to grow fastest of all, reaching

their adult size long before you've reached your adult height. To some girls, it can seem as if their feet are growing out of control—and that they will have huge feet or feet way too long for some- one of their height.

Fortu- nately, this doesn't happen. Although your feet grow fastest, they also stop growing first. When you get taller, your feet will be back in proportion to your height.

The growth spurt may seem to be going on forever when it's happen- ing, but in reality it doesn't last for very long—usually only a year or less. Still, that means adjusting to a lot of changes over a relatively short time, something that can be pretty confusing.

While you will probably keep growing a little after your growth spurt, it will be at a much slower rate. Most girls stop growing completely one to three years after they get their first period.

Body Shape (Breasts!)

In addition to getting taller, the shape of a girl's body begins to change when she enters puberty. Her hips and thighs become wider and more curvy. The most obvious change in a girl's body is that she begins to develop breasts.

As you know, the chests of little children all look the same. In both boys and girls, breasts are flat except for a small, slightly raised circle on

each side called a nipple. Sometime between the ages of eight and sixteen, a girl's breasts begin to swell and grow out from her chest. This is a sign that her breasts are developing the milk glands that will make it possible for her to nurse a baby. Fat grows around these milk glands to protect them, giving breasts their adult shape.

This doesn't happen all at once, of course. At first, only the area around the nipple begins to stick out. The nipple feels harder and is sometimes a little tender. Often, one breast starts growing before the other. For girls who don't know that this is perfectly normal, the fact that one breast is growing when the other is not can be really scary! They may fear that there is something wrong and that they are going to end up with only one breast. That's why it's important to remember that the other breast will start growing soon. Within a short time, it will catch up with the breast that began developing first.

When Will It Happen?

Many girls are concerned about when their breasts will start to develop. Although most girls are between nine and fourteen when this happens, some are a little younger and some a little older when their breasts first begin to grow. Girls whose breasts start developing when they are nine or ten often don't feel ready yet and aren't too happy about this. On the

other hand, girls who don't start developing until long after their friends frequently feel left out. It helps to know that by the time girls are sixteen or seventeen, all of them will have gotten their breasts.

You might think that girls whose breasts begin developing at a younger age will have bigger breasts than girls whose breasts don't start growing until they are older. Actually, this isn't so. There's no connection between how old a girl is when her breasts begin to develop and how big they eventually become.

Breasts are a very big deal in American culture, and something people pay a lot of attention to. Since they are an obvious sign that a young girl is growing up, many girls feel proud when their breasts start to develop. Sometimes, girls whose breasts haven't started to grow are a little envious of those who already have them and wish that their own would hurry up and appear.

On the other hand, all the attention paid to breasts makes other girls feel self-conscious when their breasts begin to develop. Every now and then, it seems as if the whole world is staring at their chests. Many girls have both feelings—happy they are getting breasts but a little uncomfortable that they're so noticeable.

Besides feeling self-conscious about the fact that they are developing breasts, girls often worry about whether their breasts are the "right" size or whether they look OK. Even if they like their breasts, they may think their hips or some other part of their bodies have become too big or perhaps not big enough. If they decide for some reason that their bodies aren't perfect, they may feel unhappy and unattractive.

Try to remember that just as different colors of hair, skin, and eyes are all pretty, different body shapes are attractive too. The truth is that there isn't a "perfect" type of breasts or hips or waist that you should have, any more than there is a perfect eye color.

Hair in New Places

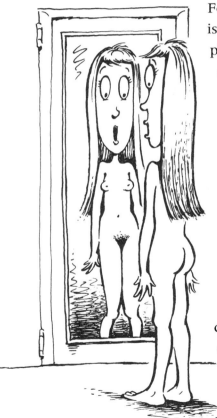

For some girls, the first sign of puberty is that they begin to grow hair in new places. One of these places is the pubic area, the place on your lower torso between your legs. During childhood, this area is hairless or has very light, unnoticeable hairs. Sometime between the ages of eight and sixteen, however, a different kind of hair begins to appear here.

Like the development of your breasts, the growth of pubic hair starts very slowly—only one or two hairs at first. It's easy to tell these new hairs from childhood hairs because they are darker, longer, and curlier. Over time, these hairs become more numerous, covering your pubic area in a kind of upside-down triangle.

If you are a blond or a redhead, you may find, to your surprise, that you have much darker pubic hair. Even if the color of your pubic hair is similar to the color of the hair on your head, it may have a very different texture. For example, girls who have straight hair on their head generally have curlier hair in their pubic area.

Along with pubic hair, hair begins to grow in the armpits. The hair on a girl's legs and sometimes on her arms becomes darker too. Less often, a girl may notice darker hairs on her upper lip as well.

Skin Changes and Perspiration

Some of the changes you probably wish weren't so visible are those that occur in the skin. After a lifetime of never having to think about their skin, many girls now find themselves examining their faces daily for pimples. For boys and girls alike, pimples are an unwelcome sign of puberty. Although a few girls are lucky enough never to have this problem, most girls' skin breaks out at least occasionally.

During puberty, the oil glands in the skin

become more active, producing greater amounts of oil. When this oil clogs a pore in the skin, it causes a blackhead. When the clogged pore gets inflamed, a pimple results. There isn't anything you can do to reduce the amount of oil your skin produces, but there are things you can do to keep pores from getting clogged. The most important one is to keep your face and hair clean. (You can find more advice on handling pimples in chapter 7.)

Like oil glands, sweat glands become more active during puberty. Not only do young people who have entered puberty perspire more than they did as children, but their perspiration begins to have an adult odor. The possibility of giving off an unpleasant smell can be a worry to both boys and girls. You may or may not want to begin using an underarm deodorant or antiperspirant to deal with perspiration odor. A deodorant eliminates odors, whereas an antiperspirant also stops perspiration. But under most circumstances, just bathing daily and wearing clean clothes are enough to keep perspiration odor in check.

Genitals

The sex organs are the parts of the body that make it possible for a person to reproduce, or have a baby. Thus they are the organs that make girls different from boys. Most people refer to the sex organs inside the body as

Girl

Boy

Girl's
Genitals

Boy's
Genitals

Fig.1

Fig.2

the internal reproductive organs, and those on the outside are commonly called the genitals. This chapter is about those on the outside.

Just as other parts of your body begin to change as you start puberty, so do your genitals. But although the changes in your genitals are certainly visible, many girls have never had a chance to look at them. It's surprising, but girls who have helped to take care of their little brothers often know much more about what a boy's genitals look like than their own.

The best way to find out what your genitals are like is to take a look for yourself. And the easiest way to do that is to hold a mirror between your legs. If this seems like a strange thing to do, it's probably because we're taught that this is a private area that should be kept covered. But

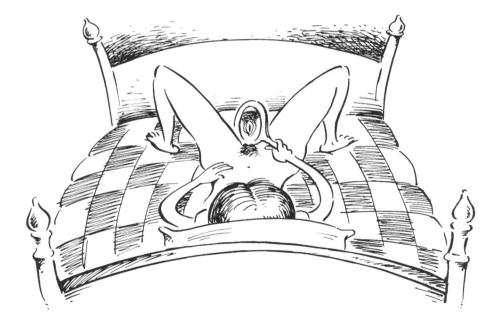

that means private from other people, not yourself! After all, a boy's genitals are private too, but no one thinks it's weird when he looks at them.

If you lie on your back with a mirror between your legs, this is what you'll see. At the top is the area where your pubic hairs first begin to grow. You're probably already familiar with this part of your body because you can see it without a mirror. During puberty, this area develops a pad of fat under the skin that makes it look a little more rounded than before.

Moving down, you'll notice that you have two folds or flaps of skin, one on each side of a narrow separation. These are called the outer lips. If you've entered puberty, you may notice that pubic hairs have started to grow here as well. The outer lips of a little girl are small, smooth, and often don't touch each other. As she enters puberty, however, the lips become fuller and grow closer together. This is to provide protection for the more delicate area underneath. With puberty, the outer lips also become darker and sort of wrinkled.

If you look inside the outer lips, you'll see another set of lips. As you might guess, these are called the inner lips. In young girls, the inner lips are small and not very noticeable, but in puberty, they begin to grow rapidly. Different girls develop differently shaped inner lips. But whatever kind you have, they will be darker and more wrinkled than the inner lips you had as a child. In many women, the inner lips

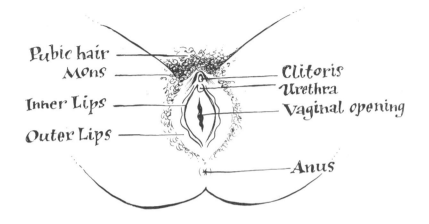

Pubic hair
Mons
Inner Lips
Outer Lips
Clitoris
Urethra
Vaginal opening
Anus

actually grow bigger than the outer lips and stick out from between the outer lips.

Now separate the inner lips. There are three very important organs protected beneath. At the bottom is an opening that leads inside your body. This is the entrance to your vagina, which we'll talk more about in the next chapter. If you are still fairly young, the entrance to your vagina may be hard to see, since it isn't very big yet, but the drawing on this page will give you an idea of where to look.

Right above the entrance to your vagina is another opening. This is your urethra, the opening through which you urinate, or pee.

Up at the top, where your inner lips join, is your clitoris. Unlike the entrance to your vagina or your urethra, your clitoris is not an opening. Instead, it's a little buttonlike bulge. The clitoris is responsible for many of the pleasurable feelings women experience when they have sex.

Finally, while you've got your mirror out, take a look at the large opening at the very bottom of your body where the two sides of your behind come together. This is the anus, the place where bowel movements come out of your body. It's not a sexual organ, so it's not part of your genitals. But it's a good thing to know about just the same.

~~~~~

Your vaginal opening leads to your internal sex organs, which have also been changing in preparation for puberty. Let's talk about these changes next.

·2·

Changes of Puberty

Those You Can't See

Just as the outside of a girl's body changes as she goes through puberty, so do the reproductive organs on the inside. You may already have seen pictures of a woman's internal sexual organs. If not, the drawing on the following page will give you a good idea of what they look like. This is what you would see if you could look inside yourself with X-ray vision.

Ovaries

The ovaries are the two roundish organs on either side of your pelvis. The ovaries contain the eggs, or ova. A baby is made from the joining of an

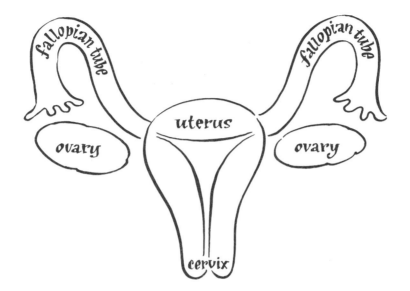

egg (called an ovum when it's only one) and a sperm, which comes from a male. This joining is called fertilization.

There are hundreds of thousands of eggs in your ovaries, and they have been there since the day you were born. But until you reach puberty, the ova don't begin to mature, or ripen, so they are unable to grow into a baby.

You may wonder what in the world you would ever do with hundreds of thousands of eggs, since you certainly don't plan to have *that* many children! Only eight or nine hundred of these ova will ever become ripe, and only a very few of those will ever be fertilized by a sperm. Thus, no matter how many children you think you may want to have, you should have more eggs than you will need.

Fallopian Tubes

The fallopian tubes are easy to spot—in the drawing they look a little like two long arms with fingers at the end, reaching out toward the ovaries. The purpose of the fallopian tubes is to guide the egg to the uterus (the next organ we'll talk about).

The "fingers" at the end of the fallopian tubes are actually fringelike projections. These projections are very important in helping a ripe egg get across the space from the ovary to the tube. By waving back and forth, they sweep the egg toward the entrance to the tube.

Uterus

The uterus is the large triangular organ between the fallopian tubes. The uterus is also called the womb, and it's the place where a fertilized egg develops into a baby.

Cervix

At the bottom of the uterus is the cervix, a knob of flesh with a small hole in the center. The purpose of the cervix is to protect the inside of the uterus. The cervix also provides an opening between the uterus and the vagina.

Vagina

The vagina is the passageway into and out of a woman's reproductive organs. By putting his penis into a woman's vagina, a man can place sperm into her body. The sperm travel up the vagina, through the cervix, into the uterus, and from there into the fallopian tubes. If there is a ripe egg in

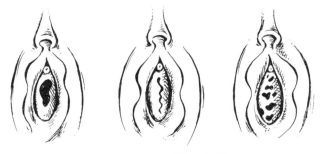

Some Hymen Variations

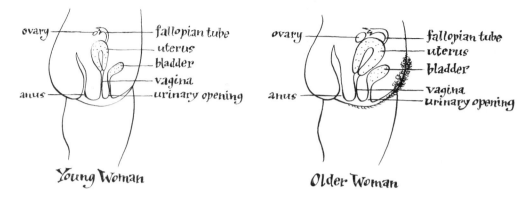

ovary — fallopian tube
uterus
bladder
vagina
anus — urinary opening

Young Woman

ovary — fallopian tube
uterus
bladder
vagina
urinary opening
anus

Older Woman

a fallopian tube at this time, it may become fertilized by the sperm.

As we'll discuss in the next chapter, your menstrual blood comes out of your body through the vagina. When a baby is being born, it travels from the uterus through the vagina to the world outside. The vagina has a protective strip of skin stretched at least partly across the vaginal opening. This skin, or membrane, is called a hymen and has a hole (or even several holes) in it.

Although all these reproductive organs are present when a baby girl is born, they grow larger as she gets older. The above drawings show the difference in the size of the ovaries, fallopian tubes, and uterus in a girl who is eleven or twelve and in a grown woman.

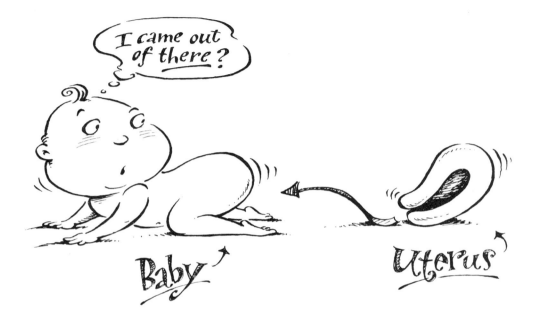

As you can see in the drawings on the previous page, the eggs must be *very* tiny if hundreds of thousands of them are to fit in the ovaries. In fact, one egg is about the size of the tip of a needle.

The fallopian tubes grow longer and wider as a girl nears puberty, but they are still smaller than you might imagine. In a grown woman, they are about four inches long but only as thick as a strand of spaghetti.

The size of the uterus is even more surprising. Even in a fully mature woman, it is only about the size of a fist. If you are wondering how a baby could possibly fit in such a small place, the answer is simple—the uterus is very elastic. As the baby grows, the uterus stretches to make room for it. Since you've seen pregnant women, you have a pretty good idea of how very much it can stretch.

The vagina is also very elastic. Most of the time, the sides of the vagina lie touching each other. But when a man and woman have sex, it stretches easily so that a man's penis can fit inside. And, of course, it stretches much wider when a baby is being born. The vagina also grows as a girl enters puberty, becoming three to five inches long by the time she is an adult.

～～～

In addition to growing, the reproductive organs shift position slightly as a girl moves from childhood to adulthood. These changes are most noticeable when you look at the body from the side, as in the pictures on page 23.

As you can see, the major change is in the position of the uterus. In a girl, the uterus is positioned straight up and down. By the time most girls have grown into women, the uterus tilts toward the front of the body. Since the bottoms of the fallopian tubes are attached to the uterus, they tilt slightly forward too.

Not every woman's uterus tilts forward, however. In some women it remains in a straight position, and in others it tips backward. These

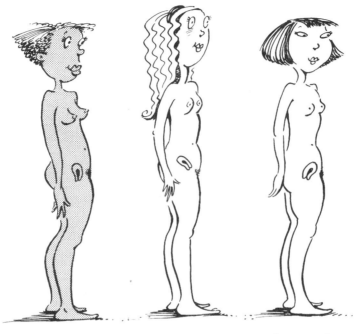

Straight   Backward Tilt   Forward Tilt

positions are perfectly normal, although not as common as a forward tilt.

Of course, you don't have X-ray eyes, so you can't see these changes occurring in your body. But when your reproductive organs have developed enough for you to have a baby, you'll get a very definite sign—you'll have your first period.

·3·

Menstruation

Menstruation, or a period, is the only outward sign of an invisible cycle that goes on in the bodies of all women. This cycle is regulated by special chemicals called hormones. Hormones are produced by glands or specialized cells in certain parts of the body, including the brain and reproductive organs. They are responsible for signaling the breasts and sex organs to develop, as well as starting the other changes of puberty. Hormones also tell the reproductive organs what to do during each part of the menstrual cycle.

The Cycle

The menstrual cycle starts once a month when a single egg ripens and leaves one of the ovaries. As you know from chapter 2, the egg then travels down the fallopian tube toward the uterus.

Meanwhile, the uterus has been preparing for the egg, just in case it becomes fertilized on its journey. The lining of the uterus develops a thick spongy cushion of blood-filled tissue to provide a fertilized egg with the food and support it will need to grow into a baby. By the time a fertilized egg enters the uterus, everything is ready for it to settle in. The

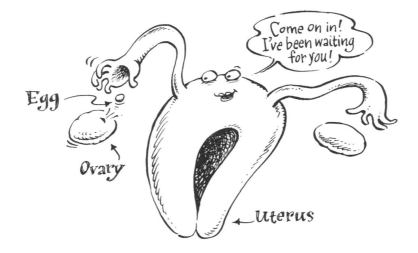

fertilized egg attaches to the lining of the uterus, starts to develop, and a pregnancy has begun.

Most often, however, the egg has not been fertilized. There can be several reasons for this. The woman may not have been sexually active. Or, the woman was using birth control; or did not have sexual intercourse at the right time, which kept the sperm from meeting the egg in the fallopian tube. Unlike a fertilized egg, an unfertilized egg does not attach to the lining of the uterus. Instead, it simply disintegrates and disappears.

Without a fertilized egg to nourish, there is no need for the thick lining of the uterus. It begins to shed slowly, dribbling out of the vagina for the next two to seven or eight days. The time when a woman is bleeding is called a menstrual period, menstruation, or just a period, for short.

This menstrual cycle occurs every month from a girl's first period until she reaches her forties or fifties. Then her ovaries begin to produce ripe eggs less frequently until they stop altogether. At that point, a woman is no longer able to have children.

When Will *Mine* Start?

That's hard to say. In the same way different girls begin to develop breasts and pubic hair at different ages, there are also differences in when girls

start to menstruate. A girl can get her first period when she is as young as eight or nine or not until she's sixteen or even seventeen, but most girls start somewhere between eleven and fourteen. Regardless of her age, however, periods don't start until *after* a girl has noticed that her breasts have begun to develop or her pubic hair has started to grow. If neither of these has happened to you yet, you probably have a while to go before you can expect your first period.

How Long Will It Last?

It's also not possible to predict how many days your period will last or how much you will actually bleed. Some girls bleed only slightly, where-as others have a heavier flow. Likewise, as noted earlier, some girls have periods that last only two or three days, while others have periods that last up to seven or eight days. Lots of times, a girl or woman will have a briefer, lighter period one month and a longer, heavier period the next. This is particularly true when you first start menstruating, until your body has had a chance to settle into a regular pattern.

Although periods come about once a month, that can mean every twenty-six days for some women and every thirty-two days for others. If you're like most women, you'll probably get your period approximately every twenty-eight days. You shouldn't expect to be that regular when you first start menstruating, however. The first year or two, while your body is getting adjusted, you may have two periods with only a week in between and then not have another one for several months. In fact, some women always have rather irregular cycles

MENSTRUAL RECORD CHART

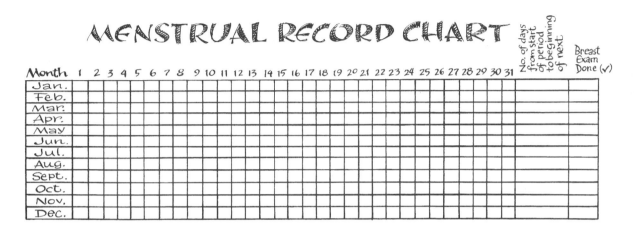

Month	1	2	3	4	5	6	7	8	9	10	11	12	13	14	15	16	17	18	19	20	21	22	23	24	25	26	27	28	29	30	31	No. of days from start of period to beginning of next	Breast Exam Done (✓)
Jan.																																	
Feb.																																	
Mar.																																	
Apr.																																	
May																																	
Jun.																																	
Jul.																																	
Aug.																																	
Sept.																																	
Oct.																																	
Nov.																																	
Dec.																																	

TYPE OF FLOW:

Normal ⊠
Exceptionally light ⊡
Exceptionally heavy ◼
Spotting ⑤

Keeping Track

As you can see, every woman has her own special cycle. The best way to learn what your menstrual cycle is like is to keep track of your periods on a calendar or chart. Starting with the first day of your period, mark the days you have menstrual bleeding. If you want, you can also make notes about which day has the heaviest flow, or how you are feeling at the time, or whatever you'd like to remember. If you keep a record of your next twelve periods or so, you'll begin to see a certain pattern. This pattern will help you know how often to expect your period, how long your periods are likely to be, and which days to be sure to carry extra pads or tampons. (We'll talk more about what to wear when you have your period in chapter 4.)

What Does A Menstrual Cycle Feel Like?

The answer to that question depends on whom you ask. Not only do different women feel differently, but the same woman can feel very differently from one month to the next.

Most women aren't aware of when an egg bursts out of the ovary. But a few can tell when this is happening because they experience a twinge or an achy feeling in their abdomen. This sensation is called mittelschmerz.

Some women feel nothing in the days before or during their periods. In a lot of ways, these women are lucky. But they do have to be especially careful to keep track of when their next period is due to begin, or they'll be caught by surprise when it starts.

Most of us, however, get signals from our bodies telling us that a period is on its way. Perhaps the most common hint that your period will start in a few days is that your breasts may feel a little more swollen or tender than usual. Since there is a tendency for the body to retain water at this time, you may also feel a little bloated.

Some women notice that they feel more emotional right before and at the beginning of their period. This can mean that they get a little cranky or find things upsetting that wouldn't ordinarily bother them. These feelings are related to hormonal changes and are part of premenstrual syndrome, or PMS for short.

"Mittelschmerz"

Often, girls may notice that their skin has a tendency to break out at the beginning of a period, so this can be another tip. These advance signals tend to lessen or disappear when your period actually begins.

Cramps

Generally, a woman feels *something* when she's having her period, at least in some months. It's a rare woman who hasn't had cramps at least once in her life, and some women have them often. Although cramps are uncomfortable, they don't mean anything is wrong. Cramps usually occur only at the beginning of a period and then taper off. For most women, they are noticeable but not bad enough to ruin their day. However, some women have cramps that are more severe. Fortunately there are many ways to deal with cramps to make them less unpleasant. (We'll talk more about handling cramps and other menstrual problems in chapter 7.) One thing's for sure, the more you learn about what to expect as your body goes through its own menstrual cycle, the easier it will be to handle having your period. And learning those things just takes a little time and practice.

·4·

What to Wear

From being around your mother or older sisters, talking to friends, or even watching TV, you probably already have some idea of the products women can wear to absorb their menstrual flow. But until you actually go to buy one for yourself, you may not realize how many choices there are! One look at a drugstore shelf crammed with different brands of maxipads, superabsorbent tampons, panty liners, regular tampons, light-day pads, tampons with applicators, tampons without applicators, pads with deodorants, pads without deodorants— and you may feel like giving up.

Don't worry! Figuring out what to wear isn't as difficult as it seems. In spite of all that variety, the choices pretty much boil down

to two: either some type of pad or some type of tampon.

Pads—or sanitary napkins, as they are also called—fit on top of the crotch of your underpants. They are made of soft cotton and usually have a plastic covering on the bottom to keep blood from soaking through and staining your clothes. Some also have plastic "wings" on the sides for added protection. On the bottom covering is a sticky strip that keeps the pad attached to your underpants. Pads come in different thicknesses for heavier or lighter periods.

Tampons are also made of an absorbent cotton, but they are shaped like a lipstick tube so they can fit inside your vagina. Some kinds of tampons come with a throwaway cardboard or plastic applicator to help you

Pads

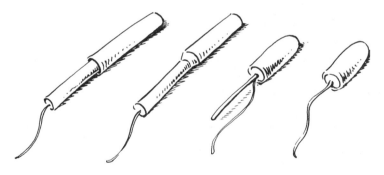

Tampons

put the tampon inside you. Others are just inserted with your finger. All tampons have a string at one end so you can pull the tampon out when it's time to remove it. Different tampons are also designed for heavier or lighter flows.

As you can see, there are some big differences between pads and tampons. But there are important similarities too. Both are easy to use. Both are comfortable. Both come in different sizes to fit your shape and different absorbencies to fit the amount of your menstrual flow. And best of all, no one can tell if you're wearing either one of them.

Which Is Better?

The answer to that is entirely up to you. If you're like most girls, you'll probably find you like one better than the other. But both have some special advantages.

For example, one reason many girls like pads is that they're so easy to use. Even a beginner can put one on with no trouble. You just take off the piece of paper covering the sticky strip, place the pad on the crotch of your underpants with the sticky strip down, press down a little so the pad sticks tightly to your underpants, and you're ready to go!

On the other hand, pads take up more space in your bag than a tampon. If you're going somewhere very dressy and are carrying a tiny

purse, it can be hard to find enough room to fit in a pad.

The biggest disadvantage of a pad is that you can't really go swimming with one on. As you can imagine, as soon as it gets wet, you have a squishy, soaked, uncomfortable glob of cotton between your legs. Even if you decide not to go in the water, a pad may be too bulky to wear with a skimpy bathing suit.

Being able to go swimming is one of the reasons many girls like tampons. Since they fit inside of you where water doesn't go, they don't get waterlogged as pads do. Also, since only the string is outside of your body,

a tampon is completely invisible and can be worn with any kind of bathing suit. Dancers and girls who play very active sports usually prefer tampons too. And because they are worn inside the body, many girls feel cleaner wearing a tampon than a pad.

A lot of girls also find tampons more convenient to carry around. In fact, some are so small they can fit in the back pocket of tight jeans without even being noticeable, and you can usually put a couple into even a tiny purse.

Finally, once you learn how to put them in, you can't even feel them at all. Many girls like the fact that tampons let them feel more like their everyday, nonperiod selves.

A Little Scary . . .

But there are some drawbacks to tampons too. Probably the biggest problem is that you have to learn how to insert them. Although putting in a tampon is really very easy, some girls find the idea a little creepy, if not downright scary. They worry that they might hurt themselves putting a tampon in or that the tampon might get lost or "go up inside them." Other girls think that virgins (girls who haven't had sex yet) aren't supposed to use tampons, or that using them means you're not a virgin any more.

Fortunately, none of these beliefs are true. You won't hurt yourself by inserting a tampon. Remember, the walls of your vagina are elastic and can expand. So even though a tampon may look too big to fit inside of you at first, it's really much smaller than your vagina.

A tampon can't get lost inside of

you because there's nowhere for it to go. If you remember from chapter 2, the hole in your cervix—the opening from the vagina to the uterus—is very little, only about the size of a match head. A tampon is much too big to fit through that space, so it can't go any farther up inside of you. It has to stay in your vagina until you decide to take it out.

Girls who are virgins usually have a hymen stretched across the opening of their vagina. That's why some people have the mistaken idea that these girls can't or shouldn't use tampons. They think the hymen has to be broken in order to insert a tampon. But when you think about it, that doesn't make sense. After all, a hymen already has a hole or several holes in it—that's how menstrual blood flows out of you in the first place. So you can use a tampon without needing to break your hymen. Another important fact that some people forget is that a broken hymen doesn't mean a girl isn't a virgin. Hymens can get broken in a lot of ways besides having sex. If a girl hasn't had sexual intercourse, she's still a virgin—whether she has an unbroken hymen or not.

Since both pads and tampons have advantages, many girls use both. They may pick tampons for a day at the beach, but choose pads for the rest of the time. Other girls who generally prefer tampons may find wearing them uncomfortable on days when they have cramps and choose pads for those times.

Practicing

Do you ever wonder what it feels like to wear a pad? One way to find out is to try one on and see. In fact, it's a good idea to do this *before* you actually need a pad, so you'll know what to expect when the time comes. Most young girls prefer a thinner pad to start with.

It's also a good idea to practice wearing a tampon at least once, even if you're pretty sure you prefer pads. That's because in emergency situations a tampon may be all that's available. It's a lot less nerve-racking to learn how to insert a tampon in your own home than when you're stuck in a strange

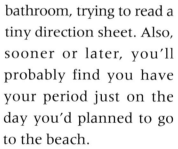

bathroom, trying to read a tiny direction sheet. Also, sooner or later, you'll probably find you have your period just on the day you'd planned to go to the beach.

Putting in a Tampon

If you do decide to practice inserting a tampon, here are some hints. First of all, be sure to buy a slender or junior size, not a regular or super size, since the slender tampons are smaller and easier to learn with.

As noted earlier, tampons may come with a cardboard or plastic applicator or be inserted with your finger.

The secret to putting in a tampon is to relax. If you're a little uptight about sticking something up your vagina, that's natural. You haven't had any experience with this before, so it may seem a little weird at first.

Ordinarily, women insert tampons while they are sitting on the toilet. You can do this if you want, but for the first time it may be easier to relax if you lie on your back on a bed.

To start, it's a good idea to wash your hands. Then remove the paper wrapping and check to make sure that the string is hanging out of the bottom of the applicator. Using your thumb and middle finger, hold on to the bottom of the larger tube, then slide the front end of the tube into your vagina. Push the tube in far enough so that your fingers touch your body.

Now push the smaller tube into the larger tube. You can use your index finger for this or a finger on your other hand. As the smaller tube slides in, it pushes the tampon into your vagina. The applicator places the tampon behind the bony ridge, so you shouldn't have to give it an additional nudge to get it in any farther. Just pull out the applicator tubes, and you're done. Although some applicators are flushable, most aren't. You'll probably need to wrap the applicator in toilet paper and toss it in a trash can. Like any tampon, these tampons are removed by pulling gently on the string.

Inserting a tampon without an applicator is a very similar process

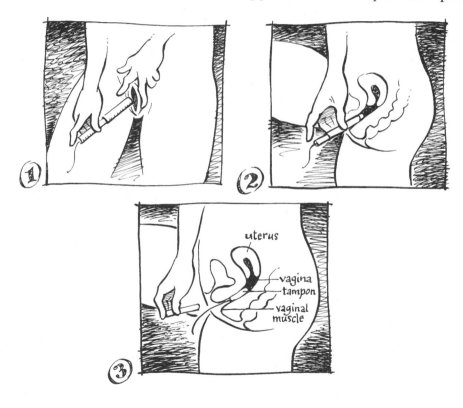

except you use your finger to push the tampon inside you instead of the small tube of the applicator. Hold the tampon between your thumb and index or middle finger. When you get the tampon in as far as it will go this way, nudge it in a little farther by pushing on the bottom of the tampon with one finger. This is to make sure you get it past the bony ridge that surrounds the opening of your vagina. When the tampon is in correctly, you shouldn't be able to feel that it's there at all. If you can feel it, you probably haven't pushed it past the bony ridge.

For some of you, inserting a tampon may be so easy that you wonder what all the fuss is about. But many girls get a little nervous the first time they try. If that happens to you, just slow down, take a deep breath, and wait a moment or two. Since tampons are harder to insert when you're tense, relaxing will make everything go much easier. Your second try should be a success.

Time for a Change

After a while, both pads and tampons have absorbed all of your flow that they can and need to be changed. In general, pads should be changed every three or four hours, even on days when your flow is light and the pad may take longer than that to get used up. Changing them frequently—even before they are completely saturated—keeps pads from developing a slight odor.

On days when your period is heaviest, you may find that your pads fill up more quickly and need to be changed more often. Fortunately, since pads are worn outside your body, you can tell if they are getting filled sooner than you expected simply by looking at them.

When you are finished with a pad, wrap it up in toilet paper and drop it in a trash can. In many public rest rooms, there are special little cans in each stall. Be careful not to flush pads down the toilet, however. While you can do this with tampons, pads are much bigger and will clog up the toilet. That's not only embarrassing for you but gross for the next person who has to use the john!

Tampons should also be changed every three or four hours. Like pads, they may have to be changed more frequently on days when your menstrual flow is heaviest. Unlike pads, however, tampons are inside your body, so you can't just take a look to make sure they aren't being used up faster than you expected. This means that you have to be careful to remember when you put the last one in. If you're worried your tampon may soak through unexpectedly, you can always wear a panty liner for extra insurance.

There's another reason for being sure you remember when you last inserted a tampon. Because you can't feel a tampon once it's in, it's easy to forget you are wearing one. This is especially true on your last day when you are hardly bleeding. Since no blood soaks through, there's nothing to remind you.

Toxic Shock Syndrome

It can be tempting to leave the same tampon in all day when your flow is very light. This is *not* a good idea, however! Leaving a tampon in for very long periods increases your chances of getting a disease called toxic shock syndrome. Toxic shock syndrome is *very, very* rare, but it is also very serious. Although anyone can get this disease—including women who are no longer menstruating and men—it occurs most often in women wearing tampons.

Although the chances are slim that you will ever get toxic shock syndrome, it's good to know what the symptoms are just to be safe. If at any time when you are wearing a tampon, you get a sudden high fever, vomiting, diarrhea, a rash that looks like a sunburn, dizziness, muscle aches, or fainting when you stand up, remove the tampon and call your doctor immediately.

Tampons themselves don't cause toxic shock syndrome. The disease is caused by a type of bacteria. But when left in too long, tampons can be a breeding ground for these germs. That's why changing your tampons regularly is so important.

Another safety precaution you should take is to use only the absorbency you really need. Since toxic shock syndrome is more likely to occur with the use of superabsorbent tampons, you shouldn't use this size unless your flow is particularly heavy. Some girls with a lighter flow think that if they use a superabsorbent tampon, they won't have to bother changing it for a whole day. As you can see, this is an *especially bad* idea!

Keeping "Fresh"

In the United States, people are extremely concerned about body odor. You probably already know about the many deodorants, antiperspirants, mouthwashes, breath mints, foot sprays, and other products designed to

make your body and breath smell better. It's hard to find people who don't rely on at least one of these products.

Although bathing, wearing clean clothes, and brushing your teeth regularly can often be enough to keep unpleasant odors away, you may still feel like using some of these products. That's OK. Even if you don't really need them, they may make you feel more confident. And unless you have an allergy to some ingredient in one of these items, they are unlikely to harm you.

But you may also have noticed advertisements suggesting that women have to be particularly worried about "staying fresh" at certain times of the month. While they don't come right out and say so, they imply that a woman's vaginal area smells bad or that she has an unpleasant odor when she is having her period. To young girls who have just started menstruating, this idea can be very upsetting. After all, the last thing they want is to have an obnoxious odor announcing to everyone that they're having their period!

Fortunately, this is one thing you *don't* have to worry about! If you are healthy, bathe daily (including washing between your legs), wear clean underpants, and change your pads or tampons frequently when you are having your period, you don't need these special products. You shouldn't worry that your genitals may have a bad odor or that other people can tell by your smell that you are menstruating. It just isn't the case!

You probably already take a bath or shower regularly and wear freshly laundered clothes, so the only thing you have to remember to do is to change your pads or tampons often, even if they aren't in danger of soaking through.

A douche is one product that's advertised as a way to keep your vagina smelling fresh. However, since your body produces natural secretions that flush out the vagina, douches are unnecessary. The only time you may need a douche is to get medication into your vagina. But a doctor will tell you if you need to do that.

·5·

Seeing a Gynecologist

A gynecologist is a doctor who has been specially trained to treat a woman's body. Therefore, this type of doctor is the best person to see whenever you have a medical question about your breasts, your sexual organs, or your period. Gynecologists can also help you with questions about birth control or about having babies. But most of all, a gynecologist's job is to help you stay healthy.

Since all adult women should be examined once a year to see if their female organs are in good shape, your mother probably already has a gynecologist that she likes. A good gynecologist takes your questions seriously and spends time with you answering them, even if you worry that they might seem silly.

54

While it's easy to understand how gynecologists can examine your breasts, you may be wondering how they examine your internal sexual organs, such as your vagina, uterus, and ovaries. The answer is simple: They look in through the entrance to your vagina. This kind of an examination is called a pelvic exam.

Your First Pelvic Exam

If you don't know what to expect, your first pelvic exam can be a weird experience. After all, it isn't every day that you have a stranger peering up your

This is a speculum. It looks worse than it feels...

vagina. Fortunately, it's a pretty simple procedure and takes only about five minutes. Although it may be a little uncomfortable, it doesn't hurt, so most girls get used to it quickly.

First, the doctor will ask you to lie on your back with your feet resting in two stirrups and your legs apart. Then he or she will put an instrument, called a speculum, into your vagina to hold the vaginal walls apart. (Remember, this doesn't hurt.) Then, with the help of a little flashlight, the doctor looks inside.

Since doctors can't see past the cervix, they have another way of examining your uterus and ovaries. They put a finger into your vagina and then press gently on your stomach with the other hand. This allows them to feel your uterus and ovaries in between. You may feel a little pressure when they do this, but it isn't painful.

Relax?

Gynecologists understand that most girls find having a pelvic exam somewhat embarrassing. They know you're probably a little nervous, and they try to help you relax. One doctor has buttons with funny sayings tacked onto the ceiling above the examining table. That way, when a patient is lying on her back being examined, she has something to distract her and make her laugh.

Some girls feel more comfortable being examined by a female gynecologist. But the most important thing is to find someone you like and feel you can talk to.

Your first period provides a great opportunity to talk with a gynecologist, and many doctors think it's a good idea to have a pelvic exam at this time as well. You should definitely start seeing a gynecologist when you begin having sex or turn eighteen—whichever comes first. Of course, whatever your age, if you feel that something might be wrong, you should ask your mom to make an appointment for you.

·6·

"is This Normal?"

Most boys and girls going through puberty worry about being normal. With all the changes happening to their bodies, many are afraid that something may go wrong. Since they don't know exactly what to expect, they spend a lot of time comparing themselves to other kids their age. They figure that if they are like everyone else, they must be OK.

The only problem with this is that "normal" and "like everyone else" are often not the same. When people say that a person's body is normal, they mean that it's healthy and developing in the way that it should. In contrast, when they use the expression "like everyone else," they don't really mean like *everyone* else, but like most of the people they know or want to be like.

Sometimes, being like your friends can seem almost as important as being normal. But there's a big difference in reality! In a year or two, many of the things that make you feel different from your friends now, such as being the first girl in your class to get your period, no longer matter. Other differences that you disliked when you were younger, such as

being the tallest girl in class, may be among the very things you like best about yourself as an adult.

On the other hand, if something going on with you is really not normal, you need a doctor's help. Sometimes, girls can be so concerned that something is wrong with them that they are too afraid to check it out with anyone else to see if it's true, particularly when it's something as personal as their period. That means a lot of girls worry needlessly about things that are perfectly natural, while others may be hiding a problem that needs medical attention.

If you are afraid that something about you isn't right, don't be afraid to talk to your mother or your gynecologist about your concern. One or the other can explain what's happening to your body. It may also help you to read about some of the worries other girls have had:

"My left breast is smaller than my right one! Everyone said that it would eventually catch up with the other breast, but it hasn't. What's wrong with me?"

It's very common for one of a girl's breasts to start developing before the other. Usually, the slower breast does catch up in size, but sometimes this isn't the case. It's perfectly normal to have breasts that are slightly different in size, or to have one breast that is somewhat lower than the other, or to have one breast pointing straight ahead while the other points a little to the side.

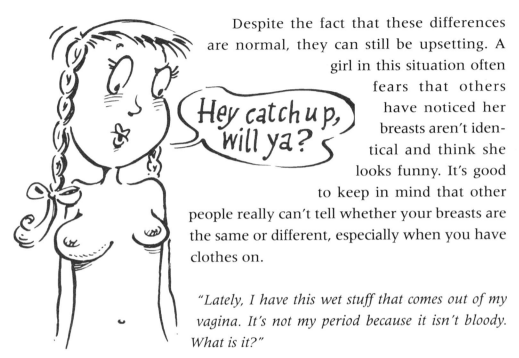

Hey catch up, will ya?

Despite the fact that these differences are normal, they can still be upsetting. A girl in this situation often fears that others have noticed her breasts aren't identical and think she looks funny. It's good to keep in mind that other people really can't tell whether your breasts are the same or different, especially when you have clothes on.

"Lately, I have this wet stuff that comes out of my vagina. It's not my period because it isn't bloody. What is it?"

As a girl develops into a woman, the lining of her vagina begins to secrete a fluid. This fluid serves a couple of purposes. It helps lubricate the vagina so that sexual intercourse is easier, and it flushes out dead cells that the vagina has shed.

Girls may first begin to notice these secretions a year or two before they have their first period. In women who are healthy, vaginal secretions are a clear, milky white, or yellowish substance that can be either slippery or rather sticky. In some women, these secretions may increase around the time of ovulation or develop a stringy consistency.

Vaginal secretions are the reason for the yellow stain that begins to appear on your underpants. Often, these secretions have a slight odor, but the smell is not unpleasant. All of this is perfectly normal and a sign that your body is maturing.

What is *not* normal is a vaginal discharge that is brownish or greenish, looks like cottage cheese, causes itching or burning, or has a sickly sweet or strongly unpleasant smell. These symptoms are a sign that you have an infection. Although a vaginal infection usually isn't serious, it's a good idea to go to a gynecologist as soon as possible. He or she can give you medication that will take care of the problem.

"I'm really worried! My period isn't just blood. There are blobs of red, jellylike stuff too. Are parts of my insides falling out?"

These blobs are a normal part of your period, although if you aren't prepared for them, they can be a little disturbing. When you have your period, your uterus is shedding dead cells as well as blood, and this mixes with mucus that is being discharged too. You're most likely to see these blobs on days when your flow is heaviest.

*"I had my first period four months ago, and my second period came the next month. But since then, I haven't had a period. I'm afraid to say anything to my mom, because I've heard that when a woman doesn't have her period, it means she's pregnant. But, **honestly**—I've never had sex! Could I be pregnant anyway?"*

Normally, the only way a woman can get pregnant is if a man places sperm inside her. And that happens only when he puts his penis into her vagina, squirts sperm at the entrance to her vagina, or has sperm on his finger and then puts his finger in her vagina. So if you haven't done any of these things, you can't be pregnant.

Being pregnant is only one of many reasons that a woman may not get her period for a couple of months. Girls are often very irregular when they first start menstruating. They may have two periods in a month and

Sperm

a half, and then not have another one for several months. It often takes a couple of years for their bodies to settle down to a regular routine. And even then, they're not likely to menstruate at *exactly* the same time each month.

Even women who are very regular often find that factors such as stress, emotional upsets, illness, or traveling make their periods come earlier or later than usual. Finally, the regular routine for some women is to be irregular, with very different amounts of time between their periods. It may be harder for them to anticipate when they will have a period, but this pattern is normal for them.

So you shouldn't worry about talking to your mother about what's going on with your periods. In fact, she may have had the same thing happen to her when she was your age and would like the chance to share her experiences with you.

*"I bleed a lot when I get my period. And I mean **a lot!** My period just doesn't seem to stop. No one I know has periods like these."*

The amount of blood in a period may look like a lot, but it's usually not as much as it seems. All together, a woman normally loses anywhere from a couple of spoonfuls of blood to a cup's worth with each period. Since it doesn't take a lot of blood to use up a tampon or pad, it can be hard to judge exactly how much you are bleeding. But if you find that you are *completely drenching* entire pads or tampons one right after the other so that you have to change them every hour for a whole day, you are probably bleeding too much and should see a gynecologist.

The length of a period and the time between periods can also vary, even a lot, and still be normal, particularly when a girl first begins menstruating. Some girls and women bleed for only a couple of days; others have periods that last seven or eight days. But when a period is this long, it should definitely be tapering off by the seventh day. And it should stop completely a day or two after that.

If your periods really aren't stopping or are coming with only a few days in between, it's important for you to see a doctor. Just as you may be finding the changes of menstruation confusing, your body may be having trouble getting things together too. Your doctor can make sure you don't lose too much blood and can get your menstrual cycle back on track.

"I thought pubic hair was just supposed to be down by your legs, but mine is growing in a line halfway up to my belly button. Plus, I'm getting a mustache! I look like a man!"

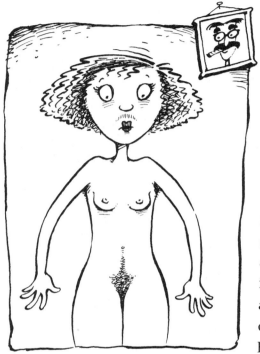

In some women, it's natural for pubic hair to grow onto the upper thighs or up toward the navel. Others may notice darker hairs appearing on their upper lip. There is nothing wrong with this, nor are these women somehow less feminine.

In our culture, however, having less body hair is often seen as more attractive. That's why many girls and women shave their legs and under their arms. Thus, while it's normal to have hair that grows a little farther up your abdomen or on your lip, you may not be too happy about it.

If you are one of these girls, there are a couple of ways you can handle this situation. One is to determine whether it's really as bad as you think. For example, the hairs on your lip that look like a man's mustache to you may be hardly noticeable to other people.

Although there are ways of removing or bleaching unwanted hair,

there are some things you definitely should not do. Attempting to shave the hair on your lip, for example, not only will leave you with a stubble but will probably make the hair grow back darker and thicker. Also, beware of using chemical hair removers on your face unless they are specifically designed for that purpose. Otherwise, you may burn or scar your skin.

    If you are troubled by the amount of hair on your face or pubic area, why not talk it over with your mother? She may have had the same concern and discovered some good solutions.

"I'm getting these yucky white lines on my breasts. It looks like my skin is starting to tear apart! What's happening?"

These are stretch marks, and they can occur any place on your body where the skin has grown very rapidly and lost some of its elasticity. Although you may not like the way they look, they certainly don't mean your skin is going to rip apart. Fortunately, stretch marks usually fade and become less noticeable with time.

Sometimes, it's not our bodies that seem abnormal, but our emotions:

"I'm in the seventh grade. Everyone else I know is dying to get their period, but **I don't want it!** *Why can't I just stay the way I am?"*

Although they may not be comfortable admitting it, lots of girls don't want to start menstruating. There can be many reasons behind their feelings. To very young girls, getting their first period way before any of their friends may seem really unfair. All of a sudden, they have to worry about cramps, counting the days between their period, carrying pads to school, and not bleeding through their clothes, when no one else they know has to bother with these things. If you're only nine, ten, or eleven years old, the idea that you are becoming a woman can be extremely upsetting and scary, especially if you don't think you've had enough time yet to be a kid.

Many older girls aren't too thrilled about the fact that their bodies are maturing either. All the talk about how they are "becoming a young woman" may seem to mean that they can no longer do some of the things that they've enjoyed up to now. Or that they are suddenly supposed to become interested in other things—like makeup and boys—when they really couldn't care less.

There's nothing you can do to slow down or hurry up the changes that are happening in your body. *But you don't have to change your feelings or your interests until you're ready!* Getting your period does *not* mean you have to become someone different. You are still you! Remember, there are all different types of women and all kinds of ways to be a woman. And you have plenty of time to figure out what kind of a woman *you* want to be.

·7·
Menstrual Problems and How to Handle Them

Very few girls experience all the menstrual problems talked about here, at least not with every period. But many will have one or two of them occasionally or even frequently. These problems tend to go away or lessen after a few years as your body gets adjusted to the changes of puberty, so just because you experience some of these difficulties at first doesn't mean you'll necessarily be stuck with them for the rest of your life. In any case, with a little practice, you'll learn how to handle the ones you do have so that they become less of a nuisance.

Pimples

Pimples don't really count as a menstrual problem since they're as likely to be an issue for boys as for girls. But many girls have a tendency to break out when they're having their period, so they are often more concerned about pimples then.

Since pimples are caused when a pore in the skin becomes clogged with oil and infected, the most important thing you can do to prevent them is to keep your skin clean. That way, there is less chance that oil will build up on the surface of your skin, and if it does, less chance that there is bacteria around to cause infection.

Keeping your skin clean means washing your face in the morning and before you go to bed. It also means keeping your hair clean. Greasy or dirty hair that touches your face adds extra oil and bacteria to your skin. Some girls whose foreheads have a tendency to break out wear bangs to hide the problem, not realizing that oily bangs may be causing the pimples in the first place. So if you have bangs, be sure to wash them frequently. Since pimples can also break out on the shoulders and back, you should keep these areas clean as well.

Every single book that talks about pimples advises teenagers not to pick at them or to pop them because this may leave permanent scars. And every single one of these books is right! But many kids continue to pop pimples anyway. Although this is a bad practice, if you're determined to do it, at least wash your hands and face (or wherever the pimple is) first.

As you know from TV and magazine ads, there are many soaps, lotions, and creams sold to prevent pimples or help them go away. If you're bothered by breakouts, these products are often helpful.

Although most boys and girls have only mild or occasional pimples, some teenagers have more severe skin problems. If you are one of these

people, you may want to ask your parents to take you to a special skin doctor called a dermatologist. A dermatologist can prescribe stronger medications to help you deal with the situation.

The good news about pimples is that you won't have to live with them forever. They tend to occur most often between the ages of fourteen to seventeen. Usually, by the time people reach their twenties, pimples are pretty much a thing of the past.

Swollen or Tender Breasts

Some girls find that their breasts become swollen or tender around the time of their period. Usually, this is only slightly uncomfortable, but sometimes it can be painful or irritating. If you are bothered by tenderness and have small breasts that don't need much support, you may want to go without a bra on these days. On the other hand, if you have larger breasts or will be playing a sport that makes your breasts jiggle around, wearing a bra with extra support may make you more comfortable.

Cramps

Some girls and women rarely experience cramps, others have them more frequently, and a few are troubled by them almost every month. Since cramps can vary from a mild, achy feeling to severe pain, what you do about them depends on how bad you are feeling.

If your cramps are mild and last a day or less, you may be able to

just ignore them. If they make you too uncomfortable for this option, then nonaspirin pain pills, or medications designed especially for period cramps—all of which can be purchased at any drugstore—may be enough to make you feel OK and able to do the things you normally do. Warmth also helps relieve cramps, so you can try taking a long, hot bath or placing a heating pad or hot-water bottle on your stomach. Gently rubbing or massaging your abdomen may bring relief as well. You'll probably want to pick activities that are less strenuous on days when you have cramps. For example, this can be a good time to read a book or rent some videos you've been wanting to see.

Some girls find that none of these solutions seem to work, and they have painful cramps that make them feel miserable almost every month. If you are one of these girls, you know that severe cramps are a major difficulty! Only people who have never had them would be silly enough to say that you're making a big deal out of nothing or that it's all in your head. If you have monster cramps frequently, you need to go to a gynecologist, who can determine why you are having them and can give you stronger prescription medications that will help relieve the pain.

Weird Emotions

It may surprise you to know that some women actually feel more energetic and in a better mood when they are menstruating. But since they don't complain about feeling good, you're not likely to hear much about this positive aspect of having a period. What you are likely to hear about are the emotions women wish they weren't having, such as feeling sad or cranky.

Of course, if you're experiencing painful cramps, you're probably not going to be in a great mood. But sometimes women feel a little depressed, irritable, or just more emotional around the time of their period, even when there's nothing specific that seems to be causing these

feelings. They may argue more with
their friends, for example, or find
their feelings get hurt more
easily than usual. As
you know from
chapter 3, these
mood swings are re-
lated to the hormonal changes that
regulate your period.

GRRRRR

There isn't a whole lot you can do to
change the way you feel at these times, but
there are things you can do to deal with
your emotions. First, don't try to feel something that you're not. There's no law that
says you have to go around pretending to
be happy when you really feel a little sad. If,
instead of hanging out with your friends as
usual, you really just want to be alone, then
go home and listen to music or take a walk
or do whatever you feel is right for you.
You may want to explain to your friends
why you don't feel like being with them,
but that's up to you.

Second, if you know that you get overly sensitive around the time of your period, try to keep that in mind. If something upsets you, ask yourself if it's really as bad as it seems or whether your reaction might be due in part to the fact that you're having your period.

As you get used to having your period, you'll learn what to expect of your own body and feelings. You'll also discover your own best ways of handling whatever menstrual problems you happen to have. But other girls and women can also be a good source of ideas on how to cope with some of these problems. You may find that it's actually kind of fun to trade solutions with your mother, older sisters, or friends.

·8·
"What if...?"

When you first start having periods, it can seem as if you suddenly have to be on guard for all sorts of things that could be awkward or embarrassing. Some of the situations girls worry about could very well happen, while others aren't very likely. Either way, it's a relief to know ahead of time how to handle some of the things you may be concerned about, such as . . .

"What if I get my period at school?"

Except for getting your period at home, school is actually one of the better places for this to happen. That's because every nurse's

office has a supply of pads on hand for just this emergency.

How you handle getting your period at school depends on several things. If you discover your period when you go to the bathroom, you have a couple of choices. In the event there's only a small stain on your underpants, you can get a pad or tampon from the bathroom dispenser or the nurse's office, put it on, and then go back to class. On the other hand, if you've bled more than that, you may want to rinse your clothes out and wait until they've dried enough to put them back on. If, by chance, you've bled a lot and your mom is home, you may want to give her a call and ask her to bring you some clean clothes. In any case, the school nurse will give you a pass that excuses you for being late getting back to class.

On occasion, you may be in class when you discover you've gotten your period. Perhaps your underpants have suddenly become very wet or you actually felt menstrual blood dripping out. If this happens, raise your hand and ask to be excused. Then go to the bathroom and check things out.

If, for some reason, the teacher refuses to excuse you from class, *get up and go anyway*. After you are finished in the bathroom, go to the nurse's office and explain what happened. She will speak to your teacher and take care of any problems your walking out of class has caused, even if you thought you had gotten your period but were mistaken.

*"What if I bleed through to the back of my skirt or pants, **and people can see it**?"*

This happens to almost every woman at some point in her life, so it's good to know that there are plenty of things you can do. If you are wearing a sweater, sweatshirt, or long-sleeved shirt that you can take off, just tie it casually around your waist so that it covers the spot. Then go to a bathroom and get a tampon or pad. If you don't have anything to tie over the spot and you're wearing a skirt, sometimes you can just turn the skirt around so the spot is in the front, and hold your bag or books in front of it until you can get to a bathroom. Probably the most common

solution is just to ask another girl to walk behind you to the bathroom. That way no one (except her, of course) can see what has happened.

Once you get to a bathroom, you can rinse out the spot, wait until your clothes have dried enough, and then put them back on again. Or you may want to call your mother to drop off a change of clothes for you.

As an extra precaution, you may want to keep a spare pair of underpants or jeans in your locker. Finally, it's a good idea to wear darker-colored skirts or pants when you have your period, at least on days when your flow is heavier. Often, blood stains aren't even visible on dark material.

"What if I get my period unexpectedly and there isn't any way to buy a pad or tampon?"

If the flow at the beginning of your period is usually light, you probably won't have to do anything at all. Your underpants will get a little stained, but you can always wash them out later. Unless you're going to be away from home (or a drugstore) for a really long time, blood probably won't soak through to your outer clothing.

On the other hand, if there's a chance that you will bleed through your underpants to your skirt or your pants, you'll want to do something to keep that from happening. If there is a public bathroom around, you're in luck. Just fold a thick layer of toilet paper or paper towels, and place it in the crotch of your underpants as you would a pad. If you're worried the toilet paper may fall out, wrap it around the crotch to keep it in place. This will probably hold you until you get home or to someplace where you can buy supplies.

Although it's unlikely, it's possible you will get your period unexpectedly in a place where there isn't any toilet paper—like on a long hike in the woods, for example. Or perhaps your flow is very heavy at the beginning of your period, and toilet paper won't be enough to protect you until you get home. In these situations, you probably have something in your bag or on your body that would make a good emergency pad. Socks work pretty well, by the way. So do bandannas and headbands. Remember, you can always wash them out afterward.

Most important, don't forget that other girls and women can be a big help if

A Sock!

you're ever stranded without a pad or tampon. Since they've all been in this predicament at some time (or have at least worried that they will), they can all imagine what you feel. Many women carry an emergency pad or tampon with them, and even total strangers will be perfectly happy to give you one if they don't need it.

"My parents are divorced, and I spend every other weekend with my dad. What if I get my first period when I'm at his house?"

This is a good situation to plan for, since it could very well happen. If you have a dresser drawer of your own in your dad's house, a smart thing to do is to store a small box of pads or tampons there, just in case. Even if your first period doesn't come while you're at his place, chances are that a future period will, and you'll be glad you have supplies on hand.

But let's assume that you are on vacation with your father, or you don't have a place to put things permanently in his house, or you get your period before you've had a chance to store some pads. Don't panic! If you have a stepmother and you're close enough to share this concern with her, she'll be glad to help.

Even if your father lives alone or you don't want to discuss this with his wife, you still have someone you can turn to—him! It may come as a surprise to you, but fathers know a lot about menstruation. Any man who has lived with a woman for any length of time knows what periods

are, what women experience when they have a period, and what kind of supplies they need to absorb menstrual flow. They also know it's a very natural part of a woman's life.

In fact, even if you don't need your dad's help, you might still want to share with him the news that you've gotten your first period. Chances are that he'll feel flattered and happy that you're including him in this important event—even if he acts flustered or nervous. If your father seems a little uncomfortable when you tell him you've gotten your period, it's only because he hasn't had much practice dealing with you on this level and is worried that he won't respond the way you want him to.

"What if I can't get a tampon out?"

Many girls worry about this, even when they know a tampon can't get "lost" inside of them. In this case, you can relax! *Getting a tampon out is almost never a problem.* The most common fear — that the string may break off — just doesn't seem to happen. The only time you may run into difficulty is when the string has somehow been pushed into your vagina so that you can't get hold of it. And this hardly ever happens.

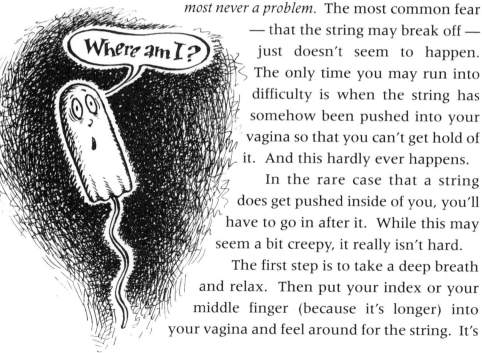

In the rare case that a string does get pushed inside of you, you'll have to go in after it. While this may seem a bit creepy, it really isn't hard.

The first step is to take a deep breath and relax. Then put your index or your middle finger (because it's longer) into your vagina and feel around for the string. It's usually easy to find. Now comes the tricky part. Because it's been in your vagina, the string is probably pretty slippery, which makes it harder to grab hold of. If you can, scoop it toward the opening of your vagina, so that you can use both your finger and your thumb to pull it out. If that doesn't work, try to twist the string around your finger so that when you pull your finger out, it won't slip off.

If you can't find the string or are having difficulty grabbing it, just go for the tampon itself. Hook your finger behind it and pull it down toward the opening of your vagina. Or you can often get hold of the tampon by squeezing it between your index and middle fingers. Sometimes, pushing down with your abdominal muscles a little will help to push it toward the entrance of your vagina.

Don't get frustrated if you don't get the tampon on the first try. Remember, it's not going anywhere, so you'll get it out eventually.

"What if I go to buy pads or tampons and the check-out clerk is a guy in my class?"

It can be embarrassing to buy supplies from someone you know. There are several ways you can handle this situation. Of course, if you have a choice of stores, you can shop in one where this isn't a problem, even if it means going out of your way. But if you live in a small town, this may be the only place available. Until you're more comfortable with things, you can ask your mother or older sister if she will pick up pads or tampons for you.

Another way to deal with this is to decide that you're not going to let it embarrass you. After all, most of the teenage and adult women in your town use these products, so chances are that this particular boy has probably already sold them to several girls that he knows. If he's cool at all, he should know that menstruating is a normal process for women. If he's a jerk, who cares what he thinks?

"What if my mother hasn't said anything to me yet about getting my period? How do I get her to talk to me?"

There may be several reasons your mom hasn't brought up this subject. If you are only nine or ten, she may not be aware that girls your age can begin to menstruate, especially if she was fourteen or fifteen when she first started. Therefore, she may mistakenly be waiting to talk to you about getting your period until you've reached the age when she thinks it's possible that this could happen to you.

If you're older, your mother may be hesitating because she isn't exactly sure how to approach the subject. Perhaps *her* mother never really talked to her or was so embarrassed when she did that it made both of them uncomfortable. Because she cares about you and realizes this is important, she's probably very concerned that she do it right. But often the more you worry about making mistakes, the harder it can be to do anything at all.

Whatever the reason she hasn't mentioned getting your period, if you'd like to be able to talk with your mom but don't know how to start, you can hand her this book and ask her if she agrees with what's written in it. Letting her know that you want to hear about her experiences can also get the ball rolling.

Finally, if your mother doesn't respond at all, remember that there are other women you know who are comfortable with this topic and who will be happy to talk with you: older sisters, cousins, aunts, coaches, and the mothers of some of your friends.

·9·

No Body is Perfect

Just because your body is developing the way it should doesn't mean that you are happy with it. In fact, if you're like most girls, you probably aren't totally thrilled with your looks. Right now, different parts of your body are growing at different rates, so it may seem like you are too small in some places and too big in others. And it doesn't help that your body probably doesn't look much like the perfect ones that you see in magazines, the movies, or on TV.

But before you start feeling bad because you don't look like a fashion model or a movie star, there's something you should know. Many of these women don't really look like that either—at least not without a lot of help. Makeup artists cover their pimples, hair stylists add extensions to make their hair fuller and longer, and fashion designers create clothes that will hide their figure flaws. Afterward, their photographs may be touched up to make their waistlines smaller or their breasts rounder. With that kind of attention, you would look great, too!

Too Thin

With all the pressure in our culture to be thin, it may seem like the skinnier you are, the better. So it's no surprise that many girls mistakenly think that they would finally be happy, if only they were thinner. Others who hope to be professional gymnasts, dancers, models, or ice skaters may be told that they would have a greater chance of success if they lost weight. As a result, some may decide to diet even if they are not overweight.

For some girls, however, trying to lose weight can lead to serious problems. You may have already heard of two eating disorders, anorexia and bulimia, that result from an obsession to be thin. Both of these conditions can cause serious health problems. And sadly, neither one makes a person more attractive.

Anorexia
People with anorexia take dieting to an extreme, refusing to eat

anything they think might be fattening. Many people with anorexia live almost completely on low-calorie vegetables like lettuce and carrots. They may also develop strange eating habits, like cutting their food into tiny pieces or refusing to eat in front of other people. Some use laxatives to help their body get rid of the little they do eat or exercise for long hours to burn up calories.

As you would expect, they do lose weight. A lot of it! So much that they look terrible. They appear to be starving because, in many cases, they are. Without a layer of fat over their bones, they look like walking skeletons. Their nails and hair become brittle, their skin becomes

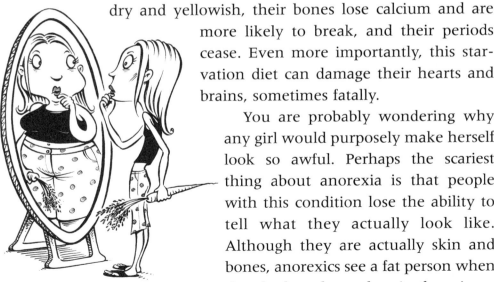

dry and yellowish, their bones lose calcium and are more likely to break, and their periods cease. Even more importantly, this starvation diet can damage their hearts and brains, sometimes fatally.

You are probably wondering why any girl would purposely make herself look so awful. Perhaps the scariest thing about anorexia is that people with this condition lose the ability to tell what they actually look like. Although they are actually skin and bones, anorexics see a fat person when they look at themselves in the mirror.

Despite the fact that they are wasting away, people with anorexia think they still need to keep their weight down. Since getting better means they will have to gain weight, they often hesitate to accept help. However, anorexia is a serious, life-threatening emotional disorder, and people with this condition need professional counseling.

Bulimia

Unlike anorexics, people with bulimia can look completely normal. Instead of starving themselves, bulimics binge on food, stuffing themselves with huge amounts at a time. After bingeing, they purge, getting rid of the food they have just eaten by making themselves throw up or by using enemas or laxatives.

Bulimics generally binge because they feel depressed, stressed, or down on themselves and eating makes them feel better, at least for the moment. But unfortunately, bingeing and purging can take over their lives, turning into a vicious cycle that they are unable to stop. Being out of control like this makes them feel ashamed and even worse about themselves.

Since they usually binge and purge in secret, it can be hard to know if someone is bulimic. But doctors and dentists can often tell because of the physical problems this causes. For example, constantly throwing up puts the teeth in contact with strong stomach acid that chews away at tooth enamel. Cavities and missing enamel on the back of the teeth are some clues that let dentists know when a person is bulimic. Repeated vomiting can also cause sore throats, swollen salivary glands, stomach ulcers, heartburn, bloating, indigestion, constipation, and irregular periods. It can even throw off the body's electrical balance, which can cause an irregular heartbeat or even a heart attack. And misusing laxatives can lead to other serious problems with digestion and may even affect the ability to go to the bathroom at all.

Like people with anorexia, girls with bulimia need professional help to overcome their emotional problems and to learn how to deal with food in a healthy way.

Too Fat

Although many girls needlessly worry that they are overweight, some are right to be concerned. More and more American children and teenagers have become obese, or seriously overweight, in the last few decades. Obesity is more than being chubby or needing to lose a few pounds. Obese people are *unmistakably* fat. Being this overweight affects their self-esteem and increases the chances that they will develop diabetes or heart problems.

There are probably many reasons why many young people are becoming obese, but two of the most important are the larger portion sizes that we have become used to eating and the fact that many children and teenagers get very little exercise.

What About You?

It can be hard to know if you need to lose or gain weight or if you're just about where you should be. And if you do need to lose weight, you may not know how to go about doing it in the right way.

One way *not* to decide whether your weight is right for you is to compare yourself to others. Your body is still developing and hasn't completely gotten its act together yet. So it isn't fair to compare yourself to models and celebrities who are adults. In fact, many women who have great figures now looked a lot like you when they were your age.

It's also not a good idea to compare yourself to your friends.

Because everyone is growing at different rates, how you and your friends look today may be very different from the way any of you will look in a year or two. Besides, bodies come in many different sizes and shapes. So what's right for a friend's body may not be right for yours.

Even a coach's suggestion that you would be better able to compete if you lost weight may not be the best advice for you in the long run. So always check with your parents first before deciding whether you need to diet.

If you are really concerned about how much you should weigh, the best person to ask is your doctor. He or she can tell you the best weight for your height and bone structure. If you do need to lose or gain weight, your doctor can help you with that as well.

Maintaining Your Best Weight

Perhaps you weigh pretty much what you should, but you'd like to stay that way. Or maybe you do need to lose a pound or two. Obviously, starving yourself or bingeing and purging are the wrong ways to control your weight. But there are some things that you can do that will help to keep your weight at a healthy level. One of the most important is to learn to stop eating when you are full. Just because you can stuff down more food doesn't mean it's a good idea. Ask yourself, "Is my stomach still hungry or do my taste buds just want more of this?" If it's your taste buds that are screaming out for more, try saving some of the food for later.

It's also important to understand why you eat. The best reason is because you are hungry. It's also fine to treat yourself to a favorite food now and then. But if you find yourself heading for the refrigerator every time you feel unhappy, remember—eating is only a temporary solution and one that may make you feel worse in the long run. A better idea is to talk to your parents or another adult that you trust about the things that are bothering you.

Also, don't forget to get exercise. You don't have to work out at a gym in order to stay in shape, but you do have to turn off the TV occasionally and move away from your computer every now and then. One of the best exercises is dancing. Walking and riding a bike are two other great ways to help maintain a healthy weight.

Finally, being healthy is very important, having a perfect body is not. There are very few perfect bodies in the world and getting one usually requires a lot of work. It's far better to spend your time and energy doing things that are more interesting—and more fun.

·10·

What Your Parents Might Like to Say to You

Just as this is an important occasion in your life, it's an important time for your parents too. Although you may not be aware of it, they are very proud of the young woman you are starting to become. But they also know that the transition from little girl to teenager isn't always easy, and they are concerned for your well-being. While they want to do their best to help make this a happy period in your life, sometimes it can be difficult to know exactly how to accomplish this.

It may surprise you, but some parents are shy when it comes to talking about their deep emotions, especially their feelings and hopes for you. Often they have a lot they want to say to you, but it's hard to get the words out. Even when your parents are comfortable with

105

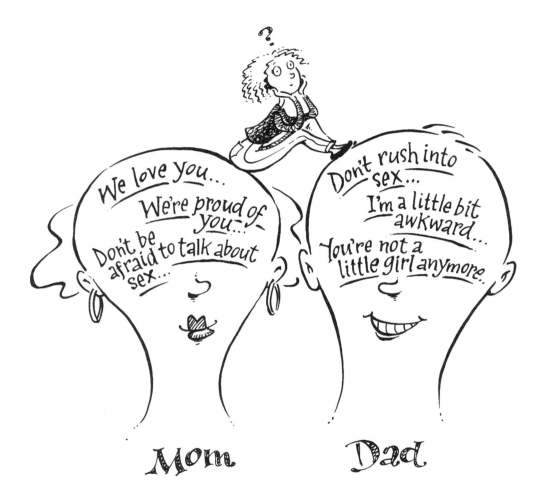

these conversations, you may be the one who gets embarrassed. So sometimes things parents may want to say—or you may want to hear—don't get talked about at all. This can be particularly true in the case of fathers and daughters.

If your parents are shy when it comes to discussing all the changes you're experiencing now (or if you're the one who's uncomfortable), you may wish you could step inside their heads and learn what they're really thinking without having to actually talk with them out loud.

Of course, that isn't possible. But you may like hearing what five parents who definitely are not shy have said to their daughters about this important time in a girl's life. Much of what they express may be similar to what your mom and dad are feeling. One way to find out is to let your parents read this chapter too and then ask them what they think about the things Lorraine, Diane, Amy, Alex, and Ron* have said.

Celebrate This Time of Your Life

Lorraine's experience when she first got her period wasn't very pleasant. As she recalls, "My feeling about having a period was one of shame. This feeling was transmitted to me by my mother, who made me feel unhappy

* Although their names are made up, these are their actual words.

about this sensitive moment. Everything she said about the experience was negative. She acted as if a girl should practically go into hiding once menstruation began!"

Diane's experience was even worse. Because she was completely unprepared, her first period almost scared her to death. "I got my period the day after I turned eleven," she says. "My mom had never told me anything. I thought babies came out of a woman's belly button! I went into the bathroom, saw blood, and got hysterical. I screamed for my mom, and she came in with a big smile on her face. That's when she told me the facts of life." Poor Diane was too shocked to be able to grasp what her mother was saying. "It was really traumatic!" she continues. "My mom was helping me with my pad, and I passed out—just passed out cold on the floor."

Many mothers who've had experiences like these are determined to handle things better with their daughters. Like all mothers, they want their girls to feel happy and proud about becoming women, not frightened and confused.

Lorraine stresses to her daughter that this is a positive event. "I've told her, 'Sweetheart, this is a celebration of life! To menstruate is a sign that you will be growing into womanhood, and that's a very wonderful thing! God has given you an important gift with menstruation—the ability to give life to another human being.'"

"We have a deal," Diane says. "When she gets her period, that's going to be a very special day. We're going to go out and celebrate! We're going to go to dinner, do something very special where we can be alone and talk. Because I feel it's a very important day for her—she's turning into a woman."

Unfortunately, Diane is one of the few women who really have a difficult time with their periods. "I just don't want her to suffer with migraines like I do and to have to start missing days from school," she says.

So although she feels good about the way she has presented menstruation to her daughter, Diane worried that the physical problems she has might have frightened her child. She was particularly concerned that her daughter would expect to have similar headaches and would dread getting her period.

Fortunately, her daughter understands that every woman is different. "You know what she said to me?" Diane continues. "'Mom, that's you. Just because you get migraines doesn't mean I'll get them. I'm a different person than you are!'"

Diane was very relieved to hear this. "When she said that, I was thrilled to death! That made me very happy! She knows that she won't necessarily have to go through what I go through."

Amy, Diane, and Lorraine all want to make sure that their daughters understand something else that's very important. Just because their daughters are physically becoming young women doesn't mean that they have to give up their childhood. As Diane puts it, "Getting your period is a *step* toward becoming a woman, toward maturity and femininity. It doesn't mean you're already there."

"Don't rush," Lorraine urges her daughter. "Enjoy your childhood, for you are still a child."

Amy agrees completely. "I want you to know that when you begin to menstruate, this is not the end of childhood," she tells her daughters. "You can play with dolls and action figures, dress up, and run around the

"Godzilla vs. Barbie"

yard playing 'pretend' if you want. Playing is an important part of being human, and we should do it all our lives. Men do! So women should not allow themselves to be told that they must stop playing."

Amy tries to prepare her girls for another aspect of becoming a woman— one that can sometimes be painful and hard to handle. During childhood, boys and girls receive relatively equal treatment. But that can change when a girl begins to mature. "So much of what I want to say to you about starting menstruation is also bound up in everything I feel you should know about being a woman," Amy explains to her girls. "Beginning to menstruate is exciting because it is physical proof of entering into adulthood, where you can imagine having the freedom to make your own decisions. But girls are often pressured to give up the equal status they had with boys during childhood."

This unequal treatment makes Amy mad! She urges her daughters not to believe that their value is less than *anyone* else's—male or female. "Women have been the shapers of the world since the beginning of humankind," she points out. "Your personal worth comes from deep inside you. Do not accept less than the respect that you deserve!"

Let's Keep Talking

Although Lorraine, Diane, and Amy find it easy to talk with their daughters, conversations about menstruation and other personal topics have been more difficult for Alex. In his case, however, the reluctance has come more from his daughters than from him. "I've tried to maintain an openness about it," he says. "And I think I'm pretty comfortable talking with them. The problem is the kind of messages kids get from other people that imply it isn't 'right' to talk about things with your parents, especially fathers. So even if parents are open, kids might not want to talk."

This bothers Alex a lot. "Teenage years are rough," he continues. "I just want to help them get through that. I think it's much more important to be able to talk about emotions than anything else."

But he also cares about the practical problems his daughters face. Although Alex is divorced and his girls live with their mother, they spend a

lot of time at his house. "I was worried that they might get their period while they were with me," he recalls. "So I bought some pads. I didn't want them to be 'undefended,' so to speak, at my house. I told them, 'I've got some pads up there for you girls, just in case.' It's funny because the response I got was, 'Oh, dad!' They pretty much shrugged it off. But I notice the package has been opened," he adds, smiling. "So they've taken advantage of it."

Save Sex for Someone Special

Even though his discussion with them was short and a little awkward, Alex felt good that his daughters knew he was thinking about the issue, concerned about making things as comfortable for them as possible, and willing to talk about the subject if they wanted to. And regardless of what his girls said (or didn't say), they were obviously glad he had been thinking about these things too.

If your mom and dad are like many parents, one topic they may want to talk with you about is sex. A lot of girls your age wonder what in the world has gotten into their parents when they bring this up! After all, having sex is probably the *last* thing on your mind right now.

It's not because your parents expect that you're going to want to have sex the minute you get your period. But however you feel and think, your body is developing the ability to have sex and make babies, so these issues will become increasingly important for you.

Your parents also know you will be experiencing a lot of pressures to be sexual in a few years and that the attitudes you form now will be important in helping you deal with these pressures. And, to be honest, they also know that when you become a teenager, you'll be less influenced by what they have to say. Since this is a very important issue, they often want a chance to talk to you about it at a time when you're more likely to listen to them.

Both Lorraine and Ron want their daughters to know that being physically able to have sex isn't enough. Sexual intercourse has a powerful emotional impact on a person, one you may not have expected or be prepared to handle. "Having sex exposes you more than just physically," Ron explains. "You expose yourself emotionally as well. At first, you will feel clumsy and awkward, uncertain and nervous. This is not something you want to experience with someone you hardly know. You can only truly enjoy sex with someone you feel at ease with, can trust, and who is committed to you. A good question to ask yourself about sex is this: Would I feel embarrassed in front of this person if I did something stupid or would he feel embarrassed in front of me? If the answer is yes, your relationship is not ready for sex."

Lorraine agrees. "Ask yourself honestly if you can deal with the outcome—mentally and emotionally—if you engage in sexual intercourse,"

she says. "There will always be pressures and you'll have questions that will make you want to explore and find out. But be wise. Put your dreams first and educate yourself. You have a lifetime to explore."

Don't Feel Pressured

Parents are well aware of how much pressure young people are under to have sex. "Part of this pressure is the steady stream of messages from magazines, TV, and movies that sexual behavior is expected from you," says Ron. "But you will also be pressured by people you know—boys and girls.

"You should know that the physical urge that boys experience is no different from the one that you feel, so any claim that they 'need' to engage in sex is nonsense.

"Understand, though, that they are under a lot of social and peer group pressure to be sexually active. This pressure is even stronger on them than it is on you. So don't be surprised if boys want to start a sexual relationship. They have been convinced that they are supposed to try this. The fact that they may try to persuade you to have sex should not necessarily be held against them. Once you have rejected a boy's attempt and he gets past the issue of sex, he may well start on the more serious business of getting to know and care about you.

"But if he continues to pressure you, you should immediately be suspicious! If he keeps pushing for sex when you say no, then he is not interested in you: he is interested in sex."

As Ron also points out, "Another source of pressure, surprisingly, will come from other girls. Often, people who feel uneasy about the fact that they are engaging in sex want reassurance that other people are doing it too. Remember, if they were all that certain of what they are saying and doing, they wouldn't be trying to make you change your behavior. They would be secure enough to let you act differently."

Because these things are often difficult for parents and daughters to talk about, Ron put what he wanted to say in a letter. That way, his daughters could read it in private. They could also keep it for when they are older and making decisions about sex, since that can be the very time when it's hardest to ask parents for advice.

Ron ended his letter by writing, "As you get older, there will be things about sex that we should discuss. I know this is a difficult subject to talk about because it is so personal, but please try to talk with me. And if you are uncomfortable, then write notes to me as I have written you."

~~~~~

Writing about your questions and feelings is a great idea, so the next few pages have been left blank for that very purpose. If your parents are giving this book to you, perhaps they'll want to write you a letter. Or maybe you'll want to write them one instead. Some of you may want to write down how you felt when you first got your period, as kind of a letter to yourself.

In any case, the next pages are just for you.

index

124